Secondary Inspections

By

Carla Rachel Sameth

Secondary Inspections

By

Carla Rachel Sameth

Nymeria Publishing, LLC

First published in the United States of America by Nymeria Publishing LLC, 2022

Nymeria Publishing

PO Box 350747

Jacksonville, FL 32235

Visit our website at www.nymeriapublishing.com

ISBN 979-8-9883332-7-2

Printed in U.S.A

For Gabriel and Milo, always. Thank you for being in my corner.

Carla Sameth's poetry collection is a thematic pendulum that sings in power and imagery where jacarandas become *the bursting of purple fireworks*. Courageous and bold, Sameth explores identity at the core of every poem. *Do you kill a child by holding or letting go?* Every day is survival in a pandemic; when your son is Black, you become a Black mother. She bores into the psyche of being othered; as a Jewish person, *You are zoo animals watched by hatred*. With a delicate balance of honesty, she is both villain and victim in love. Sameth's poetry is a rare gift of unflinching truth as she gently guides us through guilt, death, hope, and redemption in *Secondary Inspections*. We are given permission to embrace all that is beautifully human and flawed.

—Romaine Washington, author of *Purgatory Has an Address*

Table of Contents

Part II

Acknowledgments

Several of the poems in this collection have been individually published (some in different versions) in the following places:

Altadena Poetry Review: "June 2020: Alarm goes off,"

Anecdote Magazine: "The Fragility of Home"

Anti-Heroin Chic: "Bruised Arms" now called "Story of a Bruise," "Dreaming Sobriety," "Happy Face," "LA Stories: Urban Mountain Lion, South African Transplant"

Call Me [Progress] (University of Alabama): "Love Letter to a Burning World," "Unspooled" and "When You Left for Portland"

Collateral Journal: "Un-enlisted"

Hometown Pasadena: "I Do Exist" now called "Bigger Questions"

MUTHA Magazine: "Each Day," and "The Family Stories"

POETiCA REViEW: "Split Open"

Poets.org/Academy of American Poets: "Unspooled" and "Love Letter to a Burning World"

Sledgehammer Lit: "The View Changes" now called "Vista"

Spectrum: "Goodbye, Mom"

Oyedrum: "Oxytocin"

Soren Lit: "Unpacked"

Unlikely Stories Mark V: "Confessions," "Greyhound" and "Secondary Inspections"

*

"Secondary Inspections" in *The Altadena Literary Review Anthology 2020* (Shabda Press)

"Split Open" and "The Family Stories" in *The Bards of Southern California: Top 20 So Cal Poets* (Four Feathers Press 2023)

"When You Left for Portland" in *Ms. Aligned 4: Coming of Age* (Ms. Aligned Books, El Léon Literary Arts and Mañoa Books 2023)

"I Am a Woman of Almost 62 Years Old," "June 2020: Alarm goes off," "Love Letter to a Burning World," "The Fragility of Home," and "The Gods in the Middle of Election Week." in *Not So Perfect Storm, Pasadena Rose Poets Poetry Collection 2022* (Shabda Press)

"Jacaranda," now called "The Return" "Secondary Inspections," "Notes From the Place Where People Who Forget Live," "Unmoored," and "White Roses on Steroids" in *Pasadena Rose Poets Poetry Collection 2019: Reflection, Resistance, Resurrection,* (Shabda Press)

"I am a woman of almost 62 years old," in the anthology, *We Were Not Alone* (Community Building Art Works/CBAW 2021)

"*Baby In-Store Pick Up,*" "Jeannie in a Bottle," "June 2020: Alarm goes off," "The Fragility of Home," "Unspooled," "When We Could Take the Train" and "Zaftig" were included in my chapbook, *What Is Left* (dancing girl press 2021)

Part I

LOVE LETTER TO A BURNING WORLD
Southern California 2020

Praise the dark that covers us with ashes,
this morning's tears, reminding us why we cherish
the not-burning baby cry of awake, not heartbreak.

Mom, I need a hug, please,
I just can't seem to do anything right.
Raphael, the angel name, should we have birthed
a warrior instead, one who could fight the demons?

I can't say for sure I'm an addict but I'm doing too much.
He gets up, then decides he'd rather smoke,
not feeling OK right now.
I am twisted up, feel the same way. Not OK.

No, son, what you are feeling are singed embers
after six months of shutdown. Broken glass.
Murder after murder of men and women the color of your skin.
At traffic stops, in the dark, in bed, while jogging. Anywhere.

Praise the path that brought you here today, a boomerang.
Mom, I can't make it, I'm at the car repair, I need
to keep looking for someone who can fix this.
The drop like we hear in music, I hear it in his soul.

My face is wet as he leaves in a gust:
I have to meet my friends at the demonstration, I'll feel better.
More purpose. Do you kill a child by holding or letting go?
Ashes, ashes as he runs out the door.

Doesn't he know this is an emergency?
Like the blare of fire warning,
Pack your bags comes from the evacuation order.

Today his voice searing into my chest.
Praise his tears for crying with me.
Praise the seat that holds me fast.

KNOWING YOUR STORY
After Gerda Govine Ituarte

Without knowing your story
of loss—*Mother Who Carries Her Own Water*—
I couldn't face this vast expanse,
but for knowing that you survived.
You walked through fire, there is none greater.
And somehow you're whole again.

I am not there. Yet.
Fear is the engine that pushes the car that will run me over.

The gardenia from the big flowered Mexican pot, dead…gone.

Every year it bloomed before, I tucked a flower
behind my ear, or sometimes gave a fragrant gift
to a beautiful woman.

Son is sober now but
every day is still a tightrope.
He calls, *Love You Mom.*
This is the perfume that completes
the gardenia's bloom.

How many days since the kitty litter was changed?
Since I've watered my plants?
Since I've flung words onto paper?
Since I have seen my mom?
She remembers me today,
but not tomorrow.

PLAY THE TUNES

Lately, trumpet playing loses gusto—breathing
exercises, special scales I can't quite grasp, singing
notes I can't expel. It's hella hot outside. Trumpet
teacher sends practice list so long my head spins, go low,
deep-throated locomotive sounds—a grunt, a growl.

When the notes become hard to see, a doctor says my left eye
is swollen with blood droplets—stress creates a mess.
This trumpet teacher knows I'm missing delight.
Watch this young woman, Lucie Horsch,
how she becomes one with her recorder.

Melancholy reaches for me again,
I just want to play the tunes,
hear "Angel Eyes" Ella do her magic,
see the post-it—*Listen to GIMS play Hasta Luego,*
trumpet teacher's prescription.

My body begins to sway, what a heartbeat does
with a drumbeat, slip into memories of dancing
with baby in sling to Eydie Gorme y los Panchos, singing
Ojos verdes, piel canela…warm notes like chile and garlic,
of feeding my son, watching his mouth tongue the air.

SPLIT OPEN
After Natalie Diaz

What you taste
is what you crave.
Because you seek
the ripped edges,
you are drawn
to the brokenness,

the hurting scent.

Pick up the dripping carcass,
plum bruised to black
and mushy, the sopping seeds flung
from smeared papaya

gingerly touch a soft shirt's
edge to wet eyes.
Promise you'll devour
every last tendril
until the thoughts of past

come flooding in—

your mom turning down
the heat, one last goodnight,
I love you, sweet dreams,
a kiss, a promise
that no matter
how trampled
and misaligned,
her love for you
always cradled
your scattered pieces.
Drink deeply,
shirt brightly stained.
She's not
coming back.

WE USED TO ARGUE OVER HEARTS

I called my older sister over and over again whenever I ran away. The first time, six, crossing the street to the little park—but then I couldn't come back because I'd remember I wasn't allowed to cross the street by myself. I sat on a pile of leaves sniffling, imagining my sister rescuing me.

When I was a teenager, she went away to college. I'd telephone her, my complaints a steady pitter-patter or a torrent, depending on the temperature at home.

My brother taught me how to avoid recurring nightmares by focusing on the scariest moments before going to sleep. I was terrorized by dreams about "Bunny Goo," who was either a tall bald white man who wanted to take over the world or a sticky tar that got on the bathtub faucet and caused it to overflow.

My younger sister gave me imaginary sleeping pills, told me to *just breathe and think about ocean waves and Mt. Rainer, ferry boats and sunsets over Puget Sound.* She teaches meditation now. We were so young then, turning to the closet for refuge.

My dad was a high school teacher who used to say *with liberty and justice for some* when forced to recite the Pledge of Allegiance. He was my favorite dance partner, and I felt graceful on the floor with him at weddings and Bar Mitzvahs. My mom went out for Shirley Chisholm. She worked, went to school, and took care of the four of us plus my dad. Later, with almost all speech robbed by dementia, she found the words, *God that man is repulsive* when pre-2016 Trump was on television.

I miss my mom and dad, even the fights and the television blaring news, my dad's temper, his humor. His Kindness. Our stuffed animals, large, wise and plush, sat sentry, while we ran amok. *Eat a thigh instead, dark meat is juicier.* We used to argue over the hearts and gizzards; now no one wants those parts.

STORY OF A BRUISE

Purple, gold, red and yellow.
Blue too, where the elbow bends,
the space where my skin dried and flaked.

When I was six,
my teacher, Mrs. Ovens, said I
made myself itch. Some teachers tied

kids to chairs and taped mouths shut.
The screeching rip could have been Kenny's lip
or a scream from a classmate.

At 36, my arm covered with needle jabs,
tightening bands to pop out veins, unseen
by squinting eyes, I cry

use the butterfly, reserved for little children's
hard-to-find veins.
Blood mixed, ingested, taken

and given to outlast
the first trimester.
Medical voodoo transfusions.

Pooled blood, red blood cells.
Bully bruised arms,
all to bring a baby to life.

SECONDARY INSPECTIONS

A nose, a foreign look, a memory. *They just want to know if you're Jewish*,
your mom says of questions about what country you came from;
you know that you'll never pass for who you are. Everyone foreign claims your face.
City of Angels swelters, everyone here from somewhere else, still they ask,
Where were you born? and *How do you say 'Hello'?* You answer, fearing hatred.
Fear you came by naturally after strip search and secondary inspections. Not beautiful.

Go to New York—you'll be sought out, the statuesque, unapologetically beautiful
Black, Colombian woman says. Here, you're Toucan Sam, you're a Jew.
Angelenos look for an airbrushed effect, images of themselves, she says. Hatred
for your ancestral look. *You have only a slight accent, where are you from?*
Later, old Armenian men shout out greetings from their balconies, ask
questions you can't understand. You only know your strong nose on face

too ugly for years. For a girl. And you're hairy. White Angelenos seek their own face—
full lips, not too ethnic, not too angular, no rough edges. Beautiful.
Customs guards interrogate, hands grab your body. In Greece, Danish boys ask
you for towels, assume you are from Paros. A Jewish
journalist writes story, gets tweets – his beheaded caricature rises from
desire to make America white again. You are zoo animals watched by hatred.

You fear reaction to your ancestral aura. You find hidden outposts of hatred.
In the City of Angels, everyone came from somewhere else. Yet your face
looks foreign. Every day you hear, *No, where are you really from?*
No use saying you are second generation born in America, land of the beautiful.
Your mom's answer to that was always, *They only want to know if you're Jewish.*
You go with your son on a field trip, *What tribe are you?* the Cherokee guide asks.

Of course we both came across the Bering Straits, he says and doesn't ask
Where are you really from? when you answer. Shows no hatred.
From Russia, Hungary, Palestine, Turkey, you say and tell him you're Jewish.
Watch what hashtag you use, lest it shows up as a cross burned on your Facebook
page. Maybe it's true what the Colombiana says: *Go to New York, you'd be beautiful
there.* Here, your Black son looks like someone they might shoot or run from.

You look like someone who might be rounded up, asked *where from?*
A man lingering outside 7-11, looks at you both and asks,
Egyptian? Your son mimes the walk like an Egyptian dance, your beautiful
son. Later he says, *I guess there's more racism than I thought.* Hatred
spews out of a parking attendant's mouth, spits as he yells at a face
that looked a lot like my son's. KKK leader posts *Of course they're not white. Jews.*

You're looked upon with suspicion, hatred. They wonder where you're from.
Will they look at our faces, hear an unspoken word, and ask?
You wonder if you'll be beautiful, safe in New York. Jew and Afro-Jew.

LO B'SEDER

Violin. Crescent moon. Siren.
Sonata pierces.
Moon lights up.
Alarm silences serenity,
ignites night after day has finally cooled.
Walk, wine, dilutes despair.

I wish I could speak your language.
What would you say if you could?
Zeh lo tov.
Kol b'seder?
Lo, lo b'seder.
All is not well.

HER BODY IS A MAP

Her cuerpo is a field guide,
too many lessons studied,
not understood. Birdshit stains
her tangled blue-black hair,
a good place to land.
Her knuckle bears the squiggly
scar, punctured by a cardboard box
when she worked on the 22nd floor
of Mayor Bradley's LA City Hall,
Superman building. Back in the day.

Her breasts are pocked
by the teeth of her ex, Alberto,
whose incisors carved his initials,
attempting to ID her for easy retrieval.
She's seen rabid perros fight—
clawing, gnawing, piercing fur
and flesh, their marks less gruesome
than her own human scar.
Mari is carved into her innermost
left thigh, the name of her daughter
ripped away at birth.
Her flesh could not forget.

Later lines move upward,
traverse her face, her lips,
a semi-circle, shaped with a smile.
Even chasms, descent, cannot stop
this new fierce climb.

We'll name her *love*,
we'll call her *Leonara*,
an alchemist who creates new
routes with mourning doves
inked bright across her body.
Mariposas cantan, grillos vuelan,
a piquant stew of words
and colors mark her
savory rescue, her lover's
laughter covering every scar.

QUARTET OF MISTAKES

Dear Enrique,

I.   I didn't mean to be felled so quickly, so over the ledge. In love with—we'll call him Ramiro—the crazy Nicaraguan with the six kids who told me there were two and that he lived alone. But there were six and he lived with the mother of two was the real story. I want to tell you that I plead guilty based on temporary insanity, and I was, as if, a feral animal on some kind of heavy narcotic. Nothing would get in the way. This is where I made the first mistake with you, imagining you'd understand the depths, the murky, undulating swamp I fell into, swam about in, and couldn't escape from.

II.   The second mistake was when I asked you to fix my bed that was broken from fucking him so hard.

III.   Then, grandfather of all mistakes, I must never, ever, ever be pardoned from: I told you, to go, soon after you'd fixed the bed, after Ramiro called me repeatedly, and demanded that I tell him if you were there, even though I'd vowed that I would eject him like vomit from my life, when I found out about the six kids and the woman that he lived with. The one that ironed all his clothes, cooked for him, and took care of their two kids. And always kept the door open for him. I was still so afraid of running Ramiro off forever, I told you, that you had to go right away, pack all your things, hide every shred of your presence, just leave, leave, leave! It was a blackout or maybe more like a whiteout, where you can't see anything through the snow falling all around you. You left heading for the airport. You'd come to LA from Seattle where we used to live to ask me to marry you and I'd sent you away before you could say the words. No room in my swollen heart for the man who once told me he loved me by saying, *I'd like to grow old with you* after we observed an elderly woman eating in McDonalds by herself. The list is long, Enrique, all the ways you cared for me, the pork and chicken adobo, clams in ginger and chile broth, the Filipino chicken soup, the solidness of you when I came home each day from preparing hundreds of cases against batterers, hearing the stories of the women, the survivors, who were forced to eat dog shit, nipples half bitten off, and with mothers who told them that the man who did it, was the best thing that ever happened to them.

IV.   I tried to tell you I was sorry back then. And then again, later, when I visited Seattle. Perhaps slapping you on the face wasn't the right way. Perhaps it was the drama. It's no joke though, our life shredded into floating specks that couldn't be captured. Like the way Kleenex left in a pocket, then washed with pants, lands everywhere and you can never clean it up. In Seattle, I tried to tell you about my huge mistake. How you were the one I loved. You told me over and over that you could forgive me, probably even still loved me, but you couldn't trust me again. That's when I slapped you.

*

Enrique,

You were the best thing that ever happened to me, you showed me sweet, safe harbor after I read all those details in the police reports, and heard the women say no one would love them again the way those men loved them, the ones who had broken their bodies and souls into fragments.

BOTH FEET ON THE FLOOR

I'm done with trying to get you to read the book about the funny looking people who felt like they sneezed and then their bodies felt special. I'm going to tell you this once: Making love is beautiful. No, of course I'm not talking about your dad and me. No, I'm not saying we're unhappy. Yes, okay, at least four times. Pay attention or we won't stop for that butterfly net.

Making love is only beautiful if:

1. You have your college education.
2. You are financially independent.
3. The person is Jewish.
4. You're married.

No, I didn't say anything about what color they are— just that they should be Jewish. Why wouldn't you want to marry a nice Jewish boy? What? There aren't any Jews at your school?

Can't you see that making love... okay, sex. No, not with Julian, how do you know about him? He was the doctor I should have married instead of your dad. No, I didn't mean that. He was nobody. Of course, he was Jewish. No, I didn't have sex with him but...well your body does things you don't expect when you don't keep both feet on the floor. I told you that from the start. Rule number one.

If you are just broke or can't make enough money to support yourself and, well, you have, you have responsibilities. Like kids. Yes, four of them. No, you cannot do that, yes—that's what I wanted to do! Don't you think I ever wanted to leave a note for your grandmother saying *I'm leaving your four bratty grandchildren and your son for you to take care of?* Don't you? Yes, your dad is Jewish, duh, yes, we were married. For God's sake, just keep both feet on the floor.

THE RETURN

When I first arrived in Los Angeles, I was enamored
by so many things, signs that said
Miracle Mile, Koreatown or *Bungalow Heaven.*

But what turned me from a voyeur to a lover
was the bursting of purple fireworks
lining the streets every season.

No matter what had or hadn't happened—
Northridge Earthquake, another miscarriage, the day you left me,
El Niño and cars floating down lumpy cracked streets

where money wasn't spent on repair—
those jacarandas exploded into view, not just one, but all—
in South Pasadena, the Mayberry of San Gabriel Valley,

in Hacienda Heights the first spot
for those fleeing the East LA barrios,
or in West LA, where long curled tendrils

of hair adorn little Jewish Orthodox children.
They too stroll past the jacarandas.
The day I saw the bougainvillea that twisted

in and out of the jacaranda, I vowed I'd never live
without bougainvillea, that the next time I moved,
there would be bright fuchsia of years covering

the landscape in front of wherever I'd sleep.
The next year the purple blossomed,
intertwined with red, deep and unavoidable.

I felt the gift of spring, this too, my home. What was lost,
the family, the stepdaughter,
the security of the big house with the growing scarlet stunner.

This jacaranda on *this* street hugging *this* bougainvillea—
divorce never took take away the knowledge
that I too would return.

OUTPOUR

This is what I know. Today my son turns 21. Three years sober.
Longer than I've ever been. I *do* drink because I like the taste
I like to cut the edge. But I'm not that kind of person;

there are no other alcoholics in my family—rageaholics, anxiety addicts, yes,
maybe some daily pot smokers or nightly wine or martini sippers.
Dad stopped gambling after he lost honeymoon money at his bachelor party.

I've been a relationship fiend at times, stuck to tragic love.
Regrettably, I end up being *that kind of person.* Sometimes
I hide in the closet, try to conjure up the idea

of billowing clouds floating by, while sharp nails press
into my hand, digging a hole. But I drink
because I like to top the day off.

Though I'm not that kind of person
because if there are alcoholics in my family, then someone traded bottles
for rage, or the other way around. Or I am running away,

hiding in the dark. Insisting I'm not the person
that writes a rant that goes forever. And makes no sense.
Wake up. Wake up way later than planned. *Baaabe I'm sorry.*

Went to bed so late, took that pill at night, then had to take another with my coffee.
Pull myself awake. Dictate my writing into my phone. And hope the words fall
accurately. Rain is my constant, as comforting as the calm

after popping unremembered number of Ativan, drinking, crying until no more
tears can be wrung out. But a long dry spell is broken with this breakdown.
Outside the drought temporarily over. I wish for the grief to be rained

out too. Listen. I only want to say this:
I'm not the person who started the addiction
family tree. This is how you get up in the wee hours of morning.

Try to get thoughts out before the light comes in.

LA STORIES: URBAN MOUNTAIN LION, SOUTH AFRICAN TRANSPLANT
for Milo

You didn't want to come here. Los Angeles brought you down
To the basement, near Parker Center and the Déjà Vu Strip Club,
next to the new marijuana mall—where tourists take photos
and buy souvenirs while freshly-tatted dazzling dispensary girls sell
them strains with names like "Flying Monkey" and "Ganja
Goddess." Cornered but wild, like P-56, the four-year-old
mountain lion—not killed, but trapped, tagged and set free
to roam, not quite feral, uncertain of your role. You grow
gray-skinned from being locked away in the dank dark dream
of safe savannahs and freedom and foraging that won't get you
stunned. Like the coyotes that saunter brazenly, morning, noon
and night, across Pasadena lawns, you roam, restless, discontent,
wondering where the hunger will lead.

WHITE ROSES ON STEROIDS

Oh, you uncontainable white roses on steroids,
you knocked me over when I stepped out today.
The puffy pampas, Lily of the Nile,
the tall swaying purple Pride of Madeira.
Scent of sage, rosemary, jasmine, and even some vague
urine odor as I wander out to kiss the sky and whisper
thank you, thank you, thank you. The wild
unkemptness of it all is what wakes me up.

A wet Southern California winter gone amok
has saved us once again. If you began to think
it was all about smog and traffic, no work
and dying addicts, tent cities and no retirement,
think again. Look up as you walk out. Imagine
that somewhere the lone sprig
of color pokes out of the concrete,
even where you can't smell hope.

BOTH FEET ON THE FLOOR—50 YEARS LATER

Advice from Mom—
You children, all four
were my most creative act.
I just want you to be happy
and to be with someone
who loves you and treats you well.

NOTES FROM MUSIC TIME AT THE PLACE WHERE PEOPLE WHO FORGET LIVE

Love is all that I can give to you…

My mother's legs move forward and backwards forward

and backwards in perfect rhythm

while the beautiful singer sways like a Disney princess,

always singing, her bright red lips radiate a nonstop smile.

Mom's feet keep going as if she can still hear

the music even after the princess stops. From *Kiss Me Kate* to

So in Love, Mom adjusts her pace to tempo

as if dancing. Earlier she says, *not so good* when I ask her

how she is. *My kids are not ok.* Gershwin playing now, it's music time again.

Getting to know you… and

Don't sit under the apple tree with anyone else but me…

Some residents clapping now. Others slump in wheelchairs, snoring arrhythmically.

I love you for sentimental reasons. Mambo Italiano. Song ends.

One woman keeps clapping, doesn't stop, another sings loudly,

her "fellow travelers" turn and glare.

Mom asks if I have my wallet.

She wants to tip her. *Dancing Cheek to Cheek*

Mom's feet glide, as if dancing with my dad.

Peering at her feet as if she wonders how they do what they do.

        The place they live is called Connections,

                but as they lose more of themselves,

they're moved to Haven. *Heaven, I'm in heaven.*

        The singer ends with *Unforgettable*

                and the residents sway like palms.

BIGGER QUESTIONS

It's hard to hear my mom talking baby talk, I'd rather go to sleep
than think of how it went too fast, the craziness of raising a child alone
to carrying a diaper bag for my mom. No special shower thrown
in which I receive a diaper bag for my grammarian mom.

I could never get away with it: *Lie, lay, me, I.* Always corrected.
It went too fast. *We have to capture history,* she'd say.
The old people will soon be gone. The mom we knew never stopped
asking questions. Silent now, she clings to us. Who will remember

when I was lost at the zoo, a horse swallowed my arm,
right up to the elbow? I have bigger questions to ask my mom
but she has no answers. She sees scary men with red beards,
and bad boys she thinks she married after my dad died.

She sees an abusive man outside the door, insists she was raped.
How to save her from a mind gone amok? *She says that all the time,*
my older sister explains. *Of course it's not true.*
And yet for her, it is, absolutely so, the doctor tells us.

The social worker comes to interview: Time to see
if she still can't remember, *I can't tell you exactly how old I am,*
my mom finally says to the social worker.
But what I can tell you, is that I do exist.

Fairies come to rescue her since we won't take her to the "FBI Travel Store."
Go there, find my husband Booth—Booth from "Bones."
Tell him he better get over here or that's the last of him.
Today she says, *open the window.* I am happy.

She wants to see the view, I think. But instead: *Let the fairies in.*
Where's your car?
               Down there.
Let's take it. Give the fairies a rest.

DREAMING SOBRIETY

I'm like Dorothy flushed with joy,
awakening, surrounded by Aunty Em and the lot.
Yes, and you and you were there I tell
my sister, and my son, Raphael.
All three of us looking
for a rehab where we could
check in together, dancing down
the rambling road to recovery.
At the first place they interview Rafa,
my sister and I wait droopy, long hours
until I finally grab a staff person
rushing officiously by. *Tell me the truth!*
It's not our first rodeo. Why the long wait?
A snarky smell, piss yellow walls.
Lone poster of empty beach.
Yup, honestly Ma'am, the place is fallin' apart,
best keep looking. We scratch our heads,
wonder who will take all three of us.
And the money? Not seeking
equine therapy or sober surfing, but still,
we are a package deal and recovery
doesn't come "three for the price of one."
We feel the weight of inevitable failure,
awash with dingy sweat. *How about Beit T'Shuvah?*
my question pops out, munchkin-like.
The Jewish recovery synagogue with
the Rappin' Rabbi and the soulful choir
led by the lovely soprano.
They don't turn anyone away there
for lack of shekels. But I realize,
Shit, it's Friday night. Can't check in on Shabbat.
Well, now I just feel like having a drink,
I say to my older sister.
She pats me on the knee.
Go ahead, no one would blame ya.
We begin to fade – greenish sickly cast –
when our oddly un-demented mom pipes up,
(Yes, she's there too. And you. And you.)

Then she goes dark again,
her words vanishing like a dust devil
sliding into the horizon.

JUNE 2020: ALARM GOES OFF,

I clutch my wife, remember
to breathe, remember
George Floyd, remember
Christopher Ballew
21, assaulted by police
up the street, in Altadena,
remember the names,
the deaths. Nonstop.
Fear floods in, room congested.
A poet wrote me a poem
that says think of your son
when you first wake up
and I do—but terror for
the risk to his soul,
his body, his skin.
This mom's heart
tumbles, even with
my wife opening the curtain,
singing me *good morning,*
good morning, even with
wild parrots and cascading
Pasadena birdsong,
the cat kneading and purring.
Even then, I cannot calm
when my wife gets up to leave.
I see three missed calls last night—
probably just son telling me
about the latest protest.

He made me laugh
at the Highland Park march—
Mom, look. that white woman.
Full Black Panther regalia,
knee high black boots,
black coveralls and beret,
fist raised, standing in front
of that MLK mural on the wall
of that hipster coffee shop?

(Would it be her Instagram post?)
The woman, she looked at me, just said,
Your life matters.

Yes, it does, son,
and I imagine
telling him this every day,
what I've always
told him:
his life means.
But the words sink into fear,
get stuck in the throat,
legs still glued to the bed,
mind gripped by galloping thoughts.
I pull the blanket over my head.

SMELLED LIKE SEATTLE

Crunchy leaves today when you stepped out, moist, fresh
coolness. Not LA, adopted city that drips an almost
fragrant urinary scent. Eucalyptus? Or might be actual
pee. Dog, cat, human, thinned out with the sun,
occasional rain. Thankful prayer escapes lips here,
now, verdant. Allow whiff of hometown to the curtain
of comfort, surprising this age when all is supposed to come
together: the ailments, the pleasure, the refusal to grip
tightly to regrets. The willingness to look the other way,
accept how it all shook out. Leave your susto behind,
At this age, nothing surprises me, you've heard this
from the elders. Their only response— a shake of the head,
a smile or chuckle. The missing people who have died
or disappeared, the ones just let go of, like the dropping
of calendar pages from the high windows as was the custom
in LA's City Hall just before the new year. That the regrets
slink sheepishly out the back door, this is what
you wish for.

SONNET FOR A WOMAN IN FLIGHT

There are a hundred shitty ways to lose you.
Your shoulder curves taste salty sweet.
The fires, the coughing, the burning, imagined flu.
See you far away, your name in my sleep.
Don't leave me now. I've just begun to latch,
a newborn first discovering breast.
It's time for me to go, she says, alas,
I thought I wanted all of you, but with less,
the door slams shut, traps stifling air.
I have to run, for fear I lose you or
half-naked my look spells despair.
I make myself stop, the undoing you abhor.
Grab a pillow, clench it tight
or find the hot woman who loved me right.

THE GODS IN THE MIDDLE OF ELECTION WEEK
November 2020

The god of my ears listens to my son's playlists. A pandemic playlist made to keep us moving when all appeared frozen, including the arms that reached out for a hug, the lips for a kiss, the hands to touch. The election week playlist to get us through this week when I figure out what was true for so many years already, that I can't always tell him, *Everything will be ok,* but the god of his soul includes songs like, "Pray Momma Don't Cry" by Rapsody, "The Times They Are A-Changin'" by Bob Dylan, "Fight the Power" by Public Enemy and "Lockdown" with Anderson .Paak. Oh and "I Can't Breathe" by H.E.R. He tells me that he does believe he'll be OK, even went roller skating with his friends, found a pathway to the god of his heart, moving joyed-up limbs to his skating playlist, even though he says, *I am so tired of people not getting it.*

*

The god of my motherhood was with me when my son was hooked up to machines and how his heart didn't stop after swallowing 80-100 Robitussin caplets. Those times. The god of my belly remembers him floating there for nine months when all the others died long before they could become my living child. A faint scar plus this grown living one reminds me of this god, as he tells me, *Mom, I'll take you to the doctor for your appointment; I'm not afraid of needles.*

*

It is possible that the god of my eyes was with me when they found out my eye was swollen, the arteries blocked, the blood pooling from what they told me was an eye stroke, too much stress, a wake-up call. The god of trumpet playing stepped in to bring this to my attention; I started playing after a 40+ year pause and the notes were becoming more and more blurry which sent me to the optometrist, the ophthalmologist, the retina specialist who showed me the pools of blood, the blocked artery, and the swollen retina and told me about the injections I would get every 4-6 weeks, way too many times. But the god of all sweetness was there and so was my wife and son who watched the needles go in.

*

And I know the god of the shattered heart showed up too, to remind me that even if I want to say this election, all these people—whose god is white supremacy—show us that everything will *not* be ok, my son is still skating *whoosh, slide, jump, turn,* headphones on, believing in the god of hope, salty ocean breeze touching his cheek, as he wheels around and around, body moving to music, waves lapping that long shore.

WHAT HER SON KNOWS

He knows she needs him
like a parched throat
craves last drops of water.

She is cleaved, a mother
needs her son this way,
the way a hummingbird circles

the Bird of Paradise,
the way the marathon runner
sprints the last 10 yards

knowing what is at stake
towards boldest cheekbones
melting smile, lashes circling

crinkly dark eyes that hold
her heart gently, he knows
without saying, her need

that will only disappear
when she dies, and even then
he is named for two angels.

And the knowing cloaks
him as if wrapped in fleece
an awning, an oasis,

a lighthouse guides him
as he slowly sails away.

WHEN YOU LEFT FOR PORTLAND

I did not know what it might feel like when
you were ready to go out on your own.
I don't mean to the recovery house or that place in Torrance or Koreatown
with the boys from The House, or your place in Silver Lake
where we climbed the stairways and they left out free lemons.

You didn't tell me you were going, so I could not say goodbye
the way I'd planned: *Son, I know you'll have adventures, plant seeds,*
I know you dream of studying in Berlin. Beware of leftover Nazis,
new right wing white supremacists, Jew-haters though we know
they treat Black people better there than they do here.
They don't know you are an Afro-Jew so you'll hear
all the tobacco-stained spit words. Ignore this.
Keep taking photos of underpasses like you always have,
throw out old losses (I wish I could).

This is how I learned, 21, living in Mexico City: Don't trust bad men in places
you can't escape after you've drank too much Brandy Presidente,
it will be too late to run down the mountain. You might end up
on the floor, carpet engraving your head, and you'll never forget
the tacos al pastor he made you eat before it happened. I could not escape that time.

I didn't call my mom, but this is how I learned that
when your kid stops calling for a while it means
you have to find him—
it might be too late, but I would have to find, save,
comfort, rescue, hug, feed you. It wouldn't be
throwing it all in one pot Jewish chicken soup.

You'd get Filipino Chicken soup with bok choy,
chayote squash, ginger, pork, jalapeño,
what I learned to cook from my ex in Seattle,
the one who got away, the one who said,
If we had stayed together, we'd have had a bunch of children.

What I wanted was to go with you when you set out
in your new old SUV up the coast
towards my birthplace.

You called halfway there and said
Mom, I don't tell anyone where I go now.
Bravado, son, I know you had to push away.
What felt like a light shove to you scared the shit out of me
because the call dropped when you were driving. I imagined
car crashes, the unidentified body of the sweetest boy that ever lived,
the one with the long lashes my sister said I curled.

So you are fine. You're reading Ta-Nehisi Coates,
the book I gave you last week.
You told me, *Portland is the whitest city, but I found
a Black barber from Arkansas. He said the people are kind here,
only harassed him four or five times over the years.*

Still, you'll probably head to New Orleans
when productions open up again. You'll find the work
with Black costume designers in a Black city. And you'll make money,
buy a house with three or four bedrooms. One for me.

I dream of grandchildren, dream of you being small
in my arms again, dream of warm milky breath.
What I want sometimes is to go back.
What I wish for you is to go forward.

GOODBYE, MOM

Poems, we feed my mom poems. And songs. Oxygen and morphine.
Then we take away the oxygen. I think of wheat fields
that no longer sway. Of the long drive home through

Canadian prairies. Arrive at Mom's, stone silent, her body still moving,
we sing her old folk songs. Hospital vigil begins soon after, never to awake
from surgery, she lies silent. I think of my wife's long-distance quarrel

with my son, yelling through phones across countries, each in their own car,
my ears exploding with fear that the two I loved most might destroy
each other. Out by a train track, I got out of the car, alone, sat atop my torn suitcase,

no water, dead phone. Shoved a handful of Ativan, chalky waterless into mouth.
Car reversed. Time would not. Got back in, drove home towards Mom.
Sun outside hospital like the Lake Louise reflection when all felt fresh,

born again, before the fight, before Mom's silence.
Now longer, morphine steals wrinkles from her brow. My mom alive,
one more week than anyone guessed. After the harp players,

the therapy dogs, and the Reiki volunteers, we still hold court,
claim the hospital room with the Tibetan singing bowl,
the bottle of wine, the last picked tea. And flowers

all about. *I'm ready to rest* I once said to my son's dad, *when do I get to rest?*
You rest when you're dead he said. Mom resting but still breathing. Peaceful beauty.
We wait with her. Too many days spent still breathing, they are going to move her.

Hospice nurse arrives, nails so perfect, mine all chips. Mom decides.
It's a good time to die. Not to be moved.
Goodbye, Mom.

THERE IS NOTHING GENTLE ABOUT REGRET

I am a veritable hoarder,
stocking my cupboards
with overflowing boxes of
Why didn't I?
and *If only I had…*
My backyard a swamp
I wade through knee-deep,
moldy piles of *should haves*:
A house, a lover, a pregnancy, a book.

Vultures swoop in
to pick over dismembered decisions.
Where is the sweetened lemonade
you would have given to a parched friend,
telling her *you did the best you could…*
This has always been in short supply.
You might have
wrapped up in the softest quilt
you'd toss over your dearest one.
Instead, you choose
the meanest sledgehammer,
the heaviest wire cutter and pay
the toughest macha outside
True Value Hardware in Altadena,
the one with ten eyebrow piercings
and ask her
to break the lock
to your garage where
you've stored last decade's regrets.

Time to dust
them off and mourn the life
you could've lived.

But this steely-eyed sabra
surprises you. She speaks to you
in Ladino, tells you to *burn
it all down.* Drags the softest
horsehair blanket from her truck,

drapes it over your shame-scarred
shoulder and tells you,
A bright star glows
inside of you
that spells herculean,
your throttled try
that turned you upside
down and inside out.
You did the best you could.

Hineni—I am here
she paints on your heart.
Then kisses you gently
goodbye, and disappears,
a sweet-smelling dust devil.

You light a match,
toss it in,
lock the garage door,
and walk away.

LANDING AT LAX

You hollowed me out, scraped clean like a gourd,
left me without anyone to accompany me home.
I wondered if all those raw surfaces are what you wanted

me to feel. I don't. If I did, I'd be high
on top of the Golden Gate Bridge.
I'd be up there thanking the pills I swallow

when the noise grinds into mayhem.
That's what I hear when you cut me down to dead
weeds. Remember to really kill them,

you have to dig them deeply out and put poison on top.
You may have already done that.
It's the time of year when I can't bring myself to leave

the house but can't stay and day-drink with episodic television.
What once was my magical city still lurks out there.
And even though it's sunny outside. I'm left with all this. And a cat

that once rescued me after my son left for the recovery house.
Room so constricted I can't see my way clear to keeping
another creature alive. I want to cross myself off the list

and stay out of the cross-hairs of the flim-flam men-
turned-saviors who might try to rescue me. That man
at the airport moving the trash bin who said, *Come here, baby,*

let me give you a hug, is that what you need?
I took that free embrace, then wondered
if my garbage smell attracted him.

The damp rot everywhere around me.
Somehow found my way out of LAX,
that huge parking structure and yet I still went home.

CONFESSIONS

If you asked me to confess, my confession would be:
I've confessed to everything except—there is this.
I told my son I hated him, at least twice.

One time I took a bite of his food in the downtown market.
He grabbed my breast, clenched skin in fury.
My hand flew out—was there a slap?

Walking out of the market, passing a trash bin, I said he belonged
in the trash. I'd discovered my instinctive reaction
was not as a parent, but as a woman who lived

in a world of women hurt by men.
He was just a little boy though and I was his mom.
This wasn't in my parenting playbook when instinct beat out nurture.

And now that I've started, I'm sure I've got other hidden pieces
to dust off, archived, from the exhibit, "Mother's Hall of Shame."
Would it help if I said I saved his life more than once?

What tears us apart is the truth that we can't always save their lives.
We don't always make things better.
I tell you, my son, that's all I ever wanted, to make things

so much better for you than it was for us.
Generation improving on generation
but that old imprint has staying power. No way to wrest it off.

Tally up all that was lost in those tumultuous, not Norman Rockwell,
not Brady Bunch days. Like my untamed parents,
there has always been a fierce heart pounding inside me that my son

can't miss. Maybe being that parent who will always be there
is enough to clean up those stains of shame.
How much do I love you? Infinity is all.

THANKSGIVING

Before the crab stuffing and the molten greens,
the grieving turkey, crispy leg reserved
for my wife, there is this year's drink—
tamarind, tequila, lime, mint, soda, jalapeño,
and champagne. I am the eager taster, hiding
in the corner from my previously sober son.
Fix you a non-alcoholic drink? I ask jerkily
while he lurks nearby this tureen of booze.
Really, everywhere you look there's booze,
wine and beer and champagne, drinks that look
like innocent cans of soda named *spicy* or *fully loaded.*
Would you name your car, your cat, your girlfriend that?
Do what you need to do, my son, I murmur.

I know it's difficult for you, Mom, says my sweet, sweet son.
I don't need to do anything.
But sooner or later, you have to get used to it…

I remember annihilation. Addiction was in charge.
Finally stopped when he turned 18. A miracle.
Tonight, alive and well, now almost 24 years old.
Do what you like. I whisper and hide far away,
remembering those cold, cold nights in the ER.
The rolled back eyes. He smiles softly
and drinks calmly. I hide my terror
in a small box and sit down to eat.

VISTA

I tell people I'm an 18-year-old butch, a *boi,* trapped
in my 58-year-old body, or a 20-something sober young man,
like my son's friends in recovery who gather around him
on his 21ˢᵗ birthday. Then I too can say things like *cool as fuck*
or even be that. One of my son's young friends, a girl, says

Oh look your mom she's such a mom, so cool so beautiful.
Tells me, *I've wanted to meet you.*
And I want you for a daughter-in-law, I think,
though she is "just a friend," who loves my son,
as many do. A young couple arrives with their baby,

who I greedily borrow. *Look how the baby looks at your mother.*
I wanted so many more. So sure of that thing, wanting
to be a mother. Only one precious one lived. One out of eight pregnancies.

But the view changes.

And I can't quantify my unstoppable gratitude for my son—until I die,
or perhaps lose my mind. Does my mom still feel gratitude? We think
we see joy slowly lighten her face when she recognizes one of us,
her children, grandchildren, caregivers. A lone piece left of her.
Sometimes her smile matches ours. Like a gurgling baby grin

mirrors a delighted audience. Yesterday I noticed she still gulps
her coffee the same way. She who talked and mothered so much
more than we cared to listen. Today she stares blankly offering a surprise
sentence, *Yes it does,* or, *That man certainly is repulsive,*
about that buffoonish, dangerous bully who's now the president.

Years before when she could talk, she pointed to Senator Obama
See that man? Someday he'll be president.

But then the view changed.

Someday I may see some of what my mom saw in her twilight years—
fairies coming to rescue her, or "bad boys," abusive men that lurk in the dark,
who she thought she married after our father died. Television movie characters.

Booth from *Bones*. Mr. Darcy. Perhaps my delusions will also be purely my own.
Or, will I worry myself to my grave like my dad? Even though Parkinson's

hammered the nail. Today the sky beams pink, gracious clouds. The sun rises
outside my kitchen window. I'm not usually up this early. Sweet surprise.
The view after the storm that blasted through
our old scoundrel, this City of Angels. Even as I age, I can see the view change.
Me in my own body. Loving my life as it is. Embracing

my South African wife, who my son calls a badass.
Perhaps I'll plant one more tattoo on my 58-year-old vessel.
But not on the breast, since it will soon meet my stomach.

The view changes.

UN-ENLISTED

Loneliness is dropping your wife at the Coast Guard base,
when you fought your last day except those last
hours, bodies puzzle-pieced together,
deep sleep, soft blue flannel sheets.
One hand holding breast, the other, butt. Her touch comforts and possesses.

Loneliness is living winter-into-spring in Connecticut and knowing
you'll have to check for ticks on your own, like before
when you picked lice out of your long hair.
You begged your hair stylist angel to shave your head but she said
Try kerosene. My grandma used it in Puerto Rico.

And didn't you want long hair for your wedding?
The pit in your stomach grows so sour
you might actually lose weight again.
You have never been a military wife before,
but you've been lonely.

Grey and frightening, empty trailers on the dirt lot
where you live, trees that are still Northeast winter bare.
Big trash bin scrawled with the word BEER.
You hear yourself say, *I had an awesome day except
when that priest was beating his dog.*

Your wife says, *You'll be shocked when this is over.*
Spring will come like an open curtain.
Just wait for the cherry trees
Bucolic ponds privately owned.
Green. Red. Orange. The blinding.

.

IN NIANTIC, CONNECTICUT

mice make nests in car air filters, Toyota Service advisor pops out
soft mice bed, quilted with droppings. *Sometimes they come out running.*
A city dweller, I grit my teeth. Folks in rural areas

are suspicious of anyone different, Jews and queers like us.
In California, we left rodents, rats, cockroaches, fleas, termites, skunks, coyotes.
Even racists and skinheads and just plain mean people.

Here, deer carry ticks, slam into cars. Critters scramble under the house,
scratch between walls. Find a tick on the shower floor.
Smash it, watch to see if my blood spurts out.

Living near Old Lyme, I'm afraid—I've seen what disease
has done to some lives. In Connecticut, icy cold when we arrive
then blistering hot then cold again. My wife and I get along

surprisingly well, bingeing Netflix, eating Rocky Road and Kettle Korn.
But when we argue, I feel like a prisoner, arms and legs spread apart, split between
being a long-distance mama and her role as a hard-ass Coastie.

I came here with plans: write all I didn't at home, publish.
Rest as I never have. Recuperate from my life
after working since I was 12. I thought, in Connecticut I'll go

to the beach, fall in love with the view, walk miles each day,
be a beautiful kind of lonely. I'll gain 10 pounds and wear flannel,
like a "real lesbian." In Connecticut we'll have our honeymoon but

won't make love much. I'll take it all with me—the greenest green,
the sparkling water, the colors, the melancholy, still and moving.
Words I'll never find to describe the deep-set landscape, the changing light.

LOST LANGUAGE

You wish you were a robot or a butterfly or on heroin. A landing.
Something soft to fall away, to catch you. Shed the rest.
The mean words of a wife who can't hear herself.

You'd like to land in a cool saged room with mint and gardenias.
Not the dying white flowers but the one you gave to the beautiful woman
with the machete and high heels. Put the flower behind her ear.

Something that lives like a bougainvillea going from shoulder to hip.
Don't worry about words that stick, that snarl, they're foxes, not butterflies.
If you let dignity fall away, your poetry, your love songs, do they make sense?

Give up, the insane one whispers. And you wonder, is it laziness?
Remorse? Or is it the smart one that tells you, for once certain, *go away*.
Read these words out loud, they are rusted and purpled.

Blackened and blued. Snake poison. You know what to do.
Toss the words up in the air and pick the one that lands hardest across your heart.
That knocks you out. Then fucking run or you'll be run off. Stop wanting.

Stop writing. No one can read your words or understand your language.
Your strong nose is ugly again.
Go on home now.

GOLDEN OPPORTUNITY

Standing in the Huntington. I tell my friend, *I got engaged here once. Not to anyone that I married,* as I pass the "Casino" yellow roses winding around the white trellis, the sculpture garden where my toddler son once ran amok with another boy, peeing on the Great Lawn.

*

Many years ago, I received two phone calls. One from my parents telling me that my Grandmother Stella had died, then one from my boyfriend who proposed to me though it took some untangling to understand that he'd asked me to get married.

The next day we met at The Huntington Gardens, my new fiancé, a brash young man that looked like Steven Spielberg. His dad wrote for comedy television and was a mean drunk. *Carla, I just like to sit in my office and think of all the stupid people in the world,* his dad would tell me.

It was Yom Kippur and even so, we stopped for a snack at the café but I could not stop hearing my mom's voice, reminding me how wrong it was to eat out in public on Yom Kippur where all the goyim could witness our lack of respect.

We had gone there to talk about my conditions for saying "yes," and by then I really wanted a baby. Long before my son had pissed on the venerated lawn, we agreed that my timeline would be more important; after having an abortion I was desperate to make up for lost children.

*

Today, my friend and I wind our way through The Desert Garden, and into the Japanese Gardens, passing the grassy area by the nudes, the gardens near empty, early morning. Members Only hours, my son now a young adult, my friend and I masked as is the custom now. Our sons met in preschool, have survived to their twenties, but not all of the boys we know have. My older sister once said, *it turns out they are so much safer in the womb.* I didn't feel that way when I had my five miscarriages. Still, I kept repeating it over the years, as my only son got older.

*

Mom, I have bad news, my son told me two days ago. A mother knows when this will be a joke or something jagged. *Elijah died. In his sleep.* Elijah—who stood out with his warmth and kind nature—was one of the young men in my son's former recovery house. Many did find their sweetness when the walking zombiness of addiction began to rattle out of their bones. Elijah emanated so much ternura that when he relapsed and was headed for prison, a place that would consume his softness and turn him into jangly glass and broken brick, I wrote him into a character that lived in Bend, Oregon, and was Samoan and Tlingit. And not an addict. But such tenderness, he could have been my son. I think that the death demon, the carnivorous crystal meth that most likely found Elijah's vein was a phantom that couldn't be shed.

On the way out we pause to seek the scent of more yellow roses, "Sparkle and Shine" and "Golden Opportunity," some still in bloom, others wilted, already fallen.

OXYTOCIN

I.

I just can't quit you, she said, though she'd never seen Brokeback Mountain.

I taught her that line.

Knock-down feral lovemaking. Tragic love. You forget the tragedy when you're fucking
that way up against the bathroom wall in her office when no one is there.
Te quiero, te amo, te adoro.
Later, her office moved. I wish they'd torn that building down.

I remember tiny trickles of sweat dripping off my chest onto a sweet small spot
between her breasts. I remember the night we both dreamed the same dream,
of her asleep on top of me. I dreamt alone, she in bed next to him.
We could have chewed each other up into pieces or drowned
content with a thousand besitos.

II.

I remember Ramiro who I tried to leave so many times then ended up
driving south with him towards the beach, towards Mexico,
as if to flee the lies that didn't line up,
holding onto the bodies that couldn't stay unstuck.

You know that boardwalk at Redondo Beach, the pier, it just burned to the ground,
he told me as if temporarily stunned at the power of fire to destroy.
Quisiera que se queme todo, I said. Where we drank those margaritas. Where we danced,
got so wasted, wanted so much, made love in back parking lots. Burn it all down!

Tijuana where we sat by the pool, tipsy drunk enough
to forget about questions like why none of his clothes were found at his mom's apartment,
where he supposedly lived? With hands that caressed me, he fed me
camarones con limón, chile, sal y aguacate. Insatiable, I sucked it from his fingers.

Other times I couldn't eat for days.
But when oxytocin was kicking in, I was ravenous. He liked to watch me eat.
Lobster in Puerto Nuevo, en route to San Felipe just before I found out
where he really lived, met su mujer, who was my age, and looked 20 years older.

Arms crossed, thick, she recited: *el puede hacer lo que quiera contigo,*
se puede casar, pero aqui es donde siempre va a regresar.
He could come and go as he wanted—even marry someone else—
but he'd always come back to her where everything was fixed
just the way he liked it. His clothes ironed, his meals made.

I stopped eating again.

Later, I imagined the scent of his neck, cologne like sweet sweat. That last time
we ran into each other, I let him hold me, inhaled while he whispered *Mira Carlita,*
tu sabes cuanto te quiero mijita; no llores mi amor, mi cielo. Te adoro.

I imagine the first taste of heroin is like that.
Never the same high. And eventually,
it will kill you.

*

III.

Some days, I want my wife to throw me down. Do me. Like those crazy loves.
Maybe she's afraid she'll hurt me because she knows what destruction can occur.
Old wounds open jagged.

When she fits around me, we are perfect puzzle pieces. I hold her lovely breast,
we float away to sleep. I am home. But on those days when we've let little hurts
cast a shadow, I crave a little hit of that other stuff.

JEANNIE IN A BOTTLE

I envy the birds. Their excited chatter,
air of impending adventures. Their travel
plans, interrupting each other, overlapping,
bursting out with their trill, I'd like
to play my trumpet songs, missing notes,
unafraid of blending my sound with other voices
across the city. Just before I'm getting ready
to shoot up my Lysol fix, morning stretching
long, my friend Jeannie appears armed
in protective gear, gloves and mask
as if an astronaut first landing
on our porch bearing
a bouquet of fresh cut flowers,
garden roses of red and orange,
oh, and the purple. Enchanted Indigo
Veronica, fragrances of hope
float into our home. An hour later, plugged
into the screen, neck stiff I see a text.
Another friend, Felicity, *dropping off chocolate,*
don't let the cats eat it. Milo Bars from South Africa
where they are from, like my wife, Milo,
nicknamed after her love
for the chocolate. Just when I've begun
to think I would never see another
known face, day-drinking best option,
a genie in a bottle arrives and Felicidad
comes soon after.
Chocolate, garden roses,
and purple shoots, birds begin,
winding down their day. A monarch butterfly flits
across the patio. A swarm of wild parrots.
Cacophonous then gone. Momentary silence—
let us remember
the mourning doves.

WHEN WE COULD TAKE THE TRAIN

Remember when each day was either a new adventure or one you simply push mud through?
Get up, sunny again, it's Southern Cal after all. In Seattle, that meant get out and play.
Today we stay locked up in our COVID bubbles, ask me which day is the hardest to bear,
grinding to a halt each morning, wake up is a slap in face, cold water over body, get out!

Get up, sunny again, it's Southern Cal after all, in Seattle, that meant get out and play,
take the Amtrak from Union Station, ceilings as high and golden as dreams that don't end.
Grinding to a halt each morning; wake up is a slap in face, cold water over body, get out.
We are figeater beetles belly up; hard to right ourselves but we are florescent in darkness.

Take the Amtrak from Union Station, ceilings as high and golden as dreams that don't end;
remember you, two years old, pushed up against white Southern strangers' startling questions.
We are figeater beetles belly up; hard to right ourselves but we are florescent in darkness,
one man drawls, *Is that child a Negro?* I parse my response like an allergic reaction.

Remember you, two years old, pushed up against white Southern strangers' startling questions.
Another peers closely at my strong nose, olive skin, your darker tone, says, *Falafeeeel!*
One man drawls, *Is that child a Negro?* I parse my response like an allergic reaction,
next train, the Amish couple and I share stories of lost babies, before you, dear one, arrived.

Another peers closely at my strong nose, olive skin, your darker tone, says, *Falafeeeel!*
I've tried your native foods. Kind tone, but you squirm, prodded, under microscope.
Next train, the Amish couple and I share stories of lost babies, before you, dear one, arrived.
Remember when each day was either a new adventure or one you simply push mud through?

LATE

There is always the one boy left standing mournfully alone,
maybe picking his nose, humming softly

or pretending to doze. Staring as if he could set
the school fence on fire watching each car that passes,

each car that *isn't* his mom. You were that mom
that one day, maybe two days, probably more

than can be counted and perhaps the boy made marks
in the dirt to show just how many times his mom arrived

long after the goodbye song, after the others swarmed
the kids and teacher. Oh so happy, so cheery, and *how was your day*

to all the Liams, Noahs and Olivias. Yes, you were
the storm, the woman, the blistering heat wave

and Santa Ana winds dragged in, a dusty shopworn air about you,
breathless, begging for forgiveness. Oh, who to first beg pardon

and how to do penance! Surely the boy would later make you
pay in dark glances. But the real cost is what hooks in,

this late day where your son cried silently,
a full 2 hours, 26 minutes and 38 seconds late,

this day will stay forever lodged in the brain that is a minefield,
that says don't step there, that memory will take your legs off,

stop your heart. Each year you think you'll ask the question,
does he remember? At 31, you think he might not

but then you imagine a shiv into his heart one day when another
precious love leaves him waiting, igniting the explosion of memory.

THE FAMILY STORIES

This is not tragedy. You know what tragedy is, I've written
about a neck wrapped by hands, what should be called *choking*,
nose splintered into little pieces, what should be called *police brutality*.

Blood seeping down leg, more times than you want to know,
what you might call my lost children. Yes, I would have been that old lady.
So many children, I miss them all.

When I tell you I'm having a hard time, I might talk about the helicopters
over our house each night as if we are in a war zone,
but I'll assure you we are not. Though each step
home for my Black son could be a battle to secure safe passage.

Don't listen if I tell you I'm unhappy, I was crying.
Not the wails you'd hear with the big stuff,
the meat of memoir, this would be whimpers.

You must wait until I'm quiet, maybe the truth
will emerge. I asked that one time, *was it just too much?*
In my own mind, finally undone that time
I lay by the side of the bed, grasping floor.

My son had become a lost boy.
The drugs, the father he longed for in his life, me, the mother
he tired of. The world, he refused to grapple with anymore.

In my own mind, I'm incapable.
See the woman with the strong arms swinging an ax. See the woman
who fights off skinheads headed towards her sisters. See the sister

who jumps in front of her older sister when their explosive dad
comes headed for her. See how generational imprints
paint rage over pain on his body.

There are too many versions of the family stories.
Two of us claimed the same black eye
from being chased into the kidney-shaped coffee table,

the mosaic my mom made to keep
from running away and leaving it all –
the four kids, the husband, the stuck place.

All my life I've been praised for tenacity, but believe me when I tell you,
I wish I'd given up climbing the mountain sometimes.
Only once I raised the white flag, told my wife,

I just can't walk another step, gasping for air,
red-faced and damp. She pulled out dry shirts, odd snacks and warm pants,
and took me up to the top, one kiss after another, listening.

GREYHOUND

Charlotte to Savannah.
It smells like bad luck
and sorrow plus a look of too much
crystal meth and DIY tattoos.
40 years since
I've taken Greyhound.
And I just noticed
I've got old hands.

UNPACKED

Did you know? This feng shui space in the tropical breeze
of your friend's Savannah house, the big pillared porch
is for you. A tree-climber's dream, live oak trees stretching languorously,
Spanish moss, purple hydrangeas. "Rest here," your friend insists,

offers a white waffle-patterned spa bathrobe.
Did you know that the birds are calling you? When thoughts
take you far away to a land rank with regret, unraveling
obsession, and rancid fear, seek the sweet bird calls.

Return to your breath. Mothering alone all these years,
son almost lost, stepdaughter amputated.
Undone. Unblended. This is what happens to your family.
Did you know when you escape back to your writing mind,

soul and heart wholly engaged, you might not even remember
how you got here? Time will move itself. Did you know
last month, your "Coastie" wife heard from three different friends
in the Coast Guard, each story, a regurgitated acronym.

MST = Military Sexual Trauma = they destroy you, take you apart,
spit you out. Stay silent. Your fault, trauma at home, trauma abroad.
Birds sometimes talk the same language in Savannah as they do
in Pasadena, but the birds you heard in your little ship-shaped cottage

in Connecticut, those birds were entirely different. Their bright red,
two-part whistle, startled you awake, reminding you
how Los Angeles and Oakland are sex trafficking capitals of the world,
while most people assume this is another country's problem.

And some of those victims, women who have been torn apart, still live.
Alive, in their lives. Some might even be caring
for your old ones. And did you know that daily meditation
calms the heart, quiets the fears

but still you find it difficult. Did you know what gratitude
a smooth turning fan moving thick salty air will cause?
Just be in this white room with tropical sea smell in Savannah.
Hear the birds. Lush muggy gardens, thick air

gives your waddle a delicious feel. A little twist.
And did you know that by virtue of experiencing violence—
sexual assault or domestic violence, violence by authorities
like when the sheriff's deputy once broke your nose,
you are more likely to be re-victimized?

Vulnerability becomes your perfume. And not because you chose it.
You carry this knowledge, you inhabit this room
because destruction has defined you.
And you're given this place to unpack.

THE FRAGILITY OF HOME

Mom, I don't think I should see you this week.
Best friend's roommate's boyfriend's roommate—their bubble—has Covid.
When did my son float in and out of my bubble?

*

Used to be I'd introduce the music to my son that his dad and I listened to,
'70s soul and funk. I took him to see Al Green, Stevie Wonder, Earth Wind and Fire.
In kindergarten, he played in a little boy band "The Blasters" with Janice Marie Vercher
(Taste of Honey). Now he sends me a Spotify list 30 hours 19 minutes
for my wife and I to dance out pandemic blues—

House Music for the Soul, my way of describing what house music means to me.

Whirl bodies about, shoulders sway, legs move forward and back, lifting
and kicking, butt shaking. Dancing, lips turned to laughter, I think of my son.
Our tiny, cluttered living room. Pushing back the mosaic kidney-shaped coffee table.

One day I found him listening to Joni Mitchell. *This guy.* Dreamy intellectual.
And I once danced to "Ojos negros, piel canela," baby in sling.
Crinkly eyes, old café au lait face. Fireworks temperament.
Soft blankie touch. Out of eight pregnancies, he was the only one who lived.

> *One live birth.*
*

At home I hear, *I love you so, so much, Mom.* Home is where I see my baby
become a young man. A young Black man. And fear is what violates that home.
Murder happens live: George Floyd, Ahmaud Arbery, Breonna Taylor.
A running catalog of voices.

We talk about:

> Kendrick Lamar – "Alright"
> Leon Bridges – "Sweeter"
> Anderson .Paak – "Lockdown"
> Harold Melvin and the Blue Notes – "Wake up"
> Old school Gil Scott-Heron

*

I live in the house I bought when my son was young, the only house
I've owned. What does home smell like? Garlic, soy sauce, vinegar,
bay leaf, ginger, chile, Chinese five spice.
What I learned amidst Tagalog and Ilokano in South Seattle
became food for my son in LA.

I roam the Pasadena neighborhood. Wild grass comforts
even with its scent like piss. Mint floats in iced tea, sage brushes nose,
lavender cools battered soul, basil blesses our meal. Turquoise,
Provence blue, red, gold and orange, bright bold bougainvillea
colors paint our little Pasadena cottage Caribbean.

*

In the early years, baby boy sweat melted onto me, while I pushed stroller,
past Roscoe's Chicken and Waffles, past Popeyes, past Pollo Unico—
the Chinese-Peruvian restaurant. We ordered 20 chickens
to eat in nearby McDonald Park for his second birthday.
Let them see you, get to know you, my mom instructed. *Walk the neighborhood.*

Alien helicopters buzzed overhead, under siege, signal constant threat,
not-yet-groomed bathrobe-clad woman wandered muttering
They shoot people and jump into our backyards. I was a single mother,
hoped the house would be home, looking for safety.
This home grew us, and then we left.

Ten years later, I come back ashamed that starter home became
my finisher home. Now home is where I sit on patio, curse
between teeth, too many months of quarantine, where I teach
summer writing camp to teenagers on Zoom, where my wife and I breathe
in our shared space. That is what spells love.

And yet home is where loneliness crawls into my bones, stealthy
as any virus. I can't bear the compressed space anymore: some days
take to the jasmine-flecked hills, past the bags of giveaway lemons,
steep stairways of Silverlake and Echo Park, where my 24-year-old son
now lives, for socially distanced visits, masked.

61

For Mother's Day he buys me lavender iced latte and a dulce de leche muffin
oozing sweet caramel into my waiting lips.
We share muffins— but later I think of red spikes and being irresponsible.

*

Home still means birds we can't name, birds who serenade us;
we recognize the mourning doves, the wild parrots, the hummingbirds.
Others fill our ears a shared symphony. My son pops in on FaceTime.
asks, *How are you, Mom?*

He turns my question back on me when I ask,
Have you had a lot of ups and downs?

> *I have.* Home is the son and wife I know
> will softly touch my wilting heart when most needed
> and least expected.

YOU –

I want to rip out your eyeballs and smash them with my biggest boots.
I want you to see me, see me, see me. I am a mother.
I am the mother. Of the twenty-two-year-old

who I kept alive. You who robbed him. Took what you wanted,
trashed what you couldn't and now I want to mash you into pieces.
You probably have a mother, but I can't think of her now.

Think of my son, survived death more than once,
swallowing 90 pills at a time. And you broke inside of his home.
Now will he always be scavenging for safety.

His first real place with friends. More than his passport,
his IRS refund, his car and house keys, his checks.
You stole his sense of peace and security. Home.

Did you know that when you steal from a mom's son,
you take from her too? You remind us that a mom cannot
protect her child, her child, her child,

no matter how old he is; they're not even safe
in the womb. I lost so many unborn babies before him,
turns out the world is an uglier place at times. It's so fragrant

with him, out in the world but too many people want to shoot
down a Black son, son of mine.
And now you, do you know who he is? What he looks like?

He's got caramel-colored eyes, soft café au lait skin,
long dark eyelashes my sister thought I curled.
Before he started pulling them out.

A puppy dog smile. We have matching tattoos symbol
of a mother holding her child, her heart beating, beating.
We got tatted last Mother's Day. Who is your mother?

I wonder when you stopped thinking of her. Was she
on your mind that day when you came back, hopped his fence
and smashed his car, stole his passport, his identity?

He has one, has many. My son, my love, a love!
What about you? Do I really need
to rip you apart, chew you up and spit you out?

Who do you love? Why do you destroy
what won't feed you? Almost five years sober,
beginning of a career, a life, and you, you, you,

You were once a boy, someone's son, love.
I could have held you in my arms and whispered:
as much as the sun, the moon and the stars. Yes, you.

HAPPY FACE

I saw her in that Trader Joe's in Eagle Rock, her eyes teared-shiny,
one eye almost closed in a yellow-green-blue cloud. She was holding
asparagus, she was holding three bottles of Two Buck Chuck,

and chocolate almond milk. I was thinking about whiskey,
about Glen Fiddich, and the actress from Amsterdam I met
on the Greek Island of Patras, after being rescued from a burning ferry.

And how she said, *Glen Fiddich, my darling, never leave home without it*
as she pulled a bottle out of her suitcase. The woman in Trader Joe's
looked like a cornered animal, her phone summoning a jerky response

as she scrambled to answer, juggling groceries,
voice rasping out a desperate plea,
No, really, OK, alright, I'm leaving, I'm sorry, I'm on my way.

It was the kind of sorry that might paint the other eye the colors
of the rainbow. She dropped the wine bottle, and the cheap Chardonnay
slopped the floor like runaway piss. She put the asparagus

in with the bath goods and set the almond milk down gently,
almost like a baby, next to the crumpets and muffins. I wanted
to tell her, *Wait, your mask won't protect you from this hurting thing.*

She wore one, of course. A happy face. But if you saw her mauled eye,
you'd know her lips weren't turned up in a smile. And also,
there will be days when you'll go out and come home unafraid,

with so much more than you left with today. Empty-handed flights
will be a distant memory as you skip towards roasted chicken,
garlic asparagus, warm almond milk and honey or Sleepytime tea

and a shot of Glen Fiddich. I wish I'd said,
You come back someday. We'll sit safely by my fireplace
and your eyes will only be hazel.

BABY IN-STORE PICK UP

They ignore the prophets, but remind us
we must inject our Lysol, twice daily.
Tell us *We've Got Your Back.*
Woman on television ad paces back and forth across the screen,
same outfit, no mask while narrator drones,
Fidelity is here to help you through the unexpected—
But we do believe Judy Woodruff.
Each night when PBS Newshour ends, she reminds us,
Stay Safe as my wife and I wave goodbye from our sofa.

There are new ads now: *In-store pick up. Make the most
of your outdoor space while at home.*
But on our side patio, mayhem—the gardenia newly planted
wilts with the first heat wave and collapses,
drowned after a failed revival attempt.

Let this be the worst thing that happened in these times,
I tell my 96-yr-old aunt. She remembers gardenias
given as sweet-smelling corsages.
The white flower's bold and delicate scent of possibilities.

Baby in-store pick up, the screen says oddly,
my eyes see messages no one else sees,
wanting to believe the good news,
but when I go to order on Shipt
they tell me they are out; I'd wanted
so many more. No substitutions. Don't want
a kitten, puppy or baby snake.
Or even the little mice they feed the snake.

Staring at my phone waiting for answers,
I wonder how long a mother can live without
the touch of a son? What if she's one of those,
who gets sick, dies alone, his last words barely heard.
And he, too, tires of it all. How long?

That answer is not for sale. Try
the NY Times crossword puzzle. Or maybe
free things on Craigslist, if that still exists.

Anti-bacterial wipes, they're all
out of those today, too. If I could pick one up
in-store, how would I sanitize the baby?

ZAFTIG

I didn't want to leave. Returning,
I wrote poems about your Rancho Alegre,
Knowing I might not return because LA
and my circle with my son, my wife's job,
was too close to the virus's spikey
reach. Yet when I thought of comfort,
the first image was Grandma Pearl
holding me, her soft bosomy
body billowing into mine.

Melodies my heart recalls
when my brain does not, still I played those songs,
the tape with Jewish songs around the world,
in Ladino, Yiddish, Hebrew, while I rocked
and nursed my baby boy, just the two of us,
looking out over San Gabriel
Mountains, wondering what the world
would be for him. He already
was my world.

When I think of Grandma Pearl's
gentle rocking, I think of being
on your land and its nearby inhabitants:
horses, pigs, coyotes, dive-bombing swallows
you said landed in your pool,
the dogs, the hawks, the bats, the pig
down across the way. The sanctuary
you said was mine whenever
I wanted to return. I sat there
shrouded by the breeze, whispering land
reminding me rocks are perfect
for sharpening thoughts,
stilling my unmasked
mind. Inviting, succulent land,
you held me.
Zaftig.

I AM A WOMAN OF ALMOST 62 YEARS OLD,

of no special bravery.
Every day, I wake up to my wife
clutching me tightly, then singing loudly,
and the cat, once a teen mama, pounding on the door,
last night's gunshots not yet forgotten.
Turn up the sound I say,
that song about waking up and working hard each day
though I am a woman inert, until I decide
to throw off all the weighted memories—
falling down interiors, the magic elastic
that holds my unkind body
tight to my imagination,
until I step out and blow kisses
to the hummingbird, frantic, ecstatic,
or just doing its job,
circling the Bird of Paradise.

Two years older than I was when
my son, friends, and family threw
that party for me,
the trio playing songs I'd once danced to,
baby in sling, like "Piel Canela,"
the carne, the aguas, las flores,
pastel de las tres leches.
My friend Gary showed up
only to jump from a parking structure weeks later.
He'd told me, *It's been a rough year*
and I agreed, *it's been a year*
and he said, *we'll talk.*
But we never did, not really.
He only called me to tell me how proud
he was of me, my son, all we've done.
And damn him, he didn't wait for that conversation
about the obliterating fog, the deep downward slide,
the gray gray as if he were another Seattle child,
or whatever said to him,
Jump Gary, jump.

I am a woman almost 62
who once had moxie, chopped wood,
built trails, leaped in front of skinheads
who threatened me and my two sisters.
A tiny speck lost in a corner
wondering if I'll rise up and blow out to the sky
when we can finally open the doors.
62, but still the nail
that may not bend,
the mango sweet and spicy,
chile and limón that bring a mouth alive.
The lips that remember the softest kisses
billowing across continents
only to discover they were once here,
right beside me.
The skater leaping,
flying, shimmying a fountain
of joy and since I'm not gliding,
my son is. Sliding through Venice Beach
and home again to me.
I am the arms that held him,
milky sweet sweat, then opened up skyward
to the honeyed moon and the bright, bright stars.

UNSPOOLED

Sometimes I feel as if I'm undone,
a big spool of yarn
rolling down a steep hill and out into the street,
down the garbage-gathered drain.

Other times, I'm standing in front of Ramón's
apartment building in Mexico City. Remember
when I broke that bottle of Tequila Herradura.
It shattered in shards and slivers.
¡Hijole, y fue uno de los Buenos!
the doorman lamented, watching the smooth
white liquid spill onto the sidewalk. Lost.
I wonder what people would say about me
as I fall and crash to smithereens.

I want to laugh out loud when I see
I'm as solid as a snow cone.
As if I could be slurped up, tossed out or simply melt away.
As if I could be a sweetness craved, a crying child's prize
on steaming summer days.

Prescription: Wrap arms tightly
around chest, imagine freshly baked challah,
imagine a Friday night when you allow
yourself to rest your shredded senses,
and put on that white lace Brazilian dress.
Do not think of shards,
think instead of strong vigas, high
ceilings, an unobstructed view
of the Big Dipper, Leonard Cohen
carrying your darkness in his secret chords.
Sing Hallelujah.
Sing Heneni.

I am here.

Notes

"Split Open," is after Natalie Diaz's "The Beauty of a Busted Fruit."

"Unmoored," is after Gerda Govine Ituarte's poem titled, "Mothers Who Carry Their Own Water."

"Her Body is a Map" contains an inverted/revised phrase from "El Arado" and is a nod to Victor Jara.

"Unpacked," es para Mi Corazón who can't travel because she was bringing home the bacon in New London, Connecticut

Gratitude

There are so many people to thank who have contributed to these poems by inspiration, instruction, feedback, editing, sharing writing space, and encouragement including: Shuly Xóchitl Cawood, Seema Reza, Chen Chen, Eduardo C. Corral, Elline Lipkin, Ada Limón, Susan Sanders, Xochitl-Julisa Bermejo, Patricia Smith, Susan Auerbach, Colette Sartor, Neema Ejercito, Lisbeth Coiman, Maria Elena Fernandez, Abby Murray, Flint, Romaine Washington, Colette Sartor, Katie Scrivner, Andrés Jaramillo, The Bocajapa Writing Group: Kerri Kumasaka, Gerda Govine Ituarte, Manuela Gomez.

Thanks go to the organizations/members of Women Who Submit and Community Building Art Works (CBAW), and to the Carrizozo Artist-in-Residence program, notably, Paula Wilson and Joanie Malkerson.

To all those who listened to me read these poems.

To my trumpet teacher, Bill Bing, who never failed to give encouragement with the writing, horn-blowing, and life in general.

For overall love and support, thank you to: Gabriel and Milo, my sisters, Jane and SheliZ, Karen Chester, Jeannie Hooper, Melissa Pinkham, Roberta Gomez, Guillermina Alvarez, Estelle Underwood, Denise Diamond, Katya Williamson, Gale Cohen (in loving memory), Susannah Copi.

Lastly, thanks to:

My sister, Jane, for her expert consultation on cover design.

Incredible poetry coach/mentor and editor: Jennifer K. Sweeney.

Fabulous publishers from Nymeria: Kennedy Champitto and Sarah Caro.

Photo Credit: Hillary Jones

Carla Rachel Sameth is the 2022-2024 Co-Poet Laureate for Altadena, CA, and a 2023 Poet Laureate Fellow with the Academy of American Poets. She is the author of the chapbook, *What Is Left* (dancing girl press), and her memoir, *One Day on the Gold Line*, was recently reissued by Golden Foothills Press. Carla's work has been selected three times as Notable Essays of the Year in Best American Essays. A Pushcart nominee, a Pasadena Rose Poet, a West Hollywood Pride Poet, and a former PEN Teaching Artist, Carla teaches creative writing to diverse communities, including high school and university students and incarcerated youth.